IMAGES
of America

KENT

(*cover*) The train station and dam are two of the more recognizable Kent landmarks. The Kent Historical Society now owns the train station, and they operate a museum on the second floor of the building, while the Pufferbelly Restaurant occupies the first floor. The area around the dam is currently being developed as a park. (Courtesy of the Kent Historical Society.)

IMAGES
of America

KENT

Michelle Tryon Wardle

ARCADIA
PUBLISHING

Published by Arcadia Publishing
Charleston, South Carolina

Library of Congress Catalog Card Number: 2004117691

For all general information contact Arcadia Publishing at:
Telephone 843-853-2070
Fax 843-853-0044
E-mail sales@arcadiapublishing.com
For customer service and orders:
Toll-Free 1-888-313-2665

Visit us on the Internet at www.arcadiapublishing.com

CONTENTS

ACKNOWLEDGMENTS

A number of people have helped make this book possible. Thanks to Guy Pernetti, director of the Kent Historical Society, who has been supportive of this project from the beginning. Thanks also to Mary Ann Green at the Kent Historical Society, who let me in many mornings. Thanks to Cara Gilgenbach, curator of the Special Collections Department of Kent State University and her staff, including Craig Simpson, who helped find and retrieve many images for me. Thanks to John Carson, who loaned historic postcards from his personal collection. Thanks to the Board of Trustees of the Brimfield Memorial House Association for allowing me to use images from their collection. Thanks to Ron Davidson, who introduced me to the Images of America series. Finally, thanks to the many people over the years who have taken and donated photographs and postcards to repositories such as the Kent Historical Society and Kent State University Special Collections Department. I'd also like to thank my friends and family for their constant love and support, including my parents, Monica and Bernard Tryon, my brother, Daryl Tryon, and most especially my husband, Matthew Wardle.

FOREWORD

The Kent Historical Society (KHS) was formed in 1971 in an effort to save the Atlantic and Great Western Railroad Depot that was built by Marvin Kent in 1875. It is currently the home of the KHS and the Pufferbelly Restaurant. The depot overlooks the Cuyahoga River, a dam and lock from the Pennsylvania and Ohio Canal, as well as the new Heritage Park. The park restoration and preservation project was a cooperative effort of the citizens of Kent, government agencies, and advisory groups, including the KHS, all working with the Environmental Protection Agency. The Heritage Park will celebrate its opening in the spring of 2005 within a beautifully constructed river edge area. The A&GW yards are just south of the park across the river from the historic mill area. Signs that tell the history of the river and the community are located throughout the park, and a walkway lets one travel from just south of Brady's Leap to Fred Fuller Park.

The bicentennial of Franklin Mills and the City of Kent will be officially marked in 2006. As Kent begins its third century, the Kent Historical Society hopes to continue its leadership roles in the preservation, education, and celebration of our city's past, present, and future accomplishments.

The Kent Historical Society is located on the second story of the railroad depot and is currently open to the public on Wednesday and Friday afternoons or by appointment. Please visit our website for additional information at http://www.geocities.com/Heartland/Park/9580/.

Guy Pernetti
Director, Kent Historical Society

One

FRANKLIN MILLS

Before the pioneers came west to what is now Kent, the Erie and later the Iroquois people inhabited the region. The Cuyahoga River provided food and transportation for the Native tribes, as it would also for the early settlers. Captain Samuel Brady and other scouts were sent to explore the western frontier and document Native American tribes.

The land that is now Northeast Ohio belonged to the State of Connecticut, known as the Connecticut Western Reserve. After the Revolutionary War, the Connecticut Land Company formed to survey the land and sell it to settlers. Aaron Olmstead purchased Range 9, Town 3 in 1801 and named the township after his son, Franklin. Before settlers came to Franklin Township, settlers from Hudson and Ravenna built a road through Franklin, as well as a bridge over the Cuyahoga River.

In 1805, the Haymaker family moved to Franklin Township. They were the first permanent settlers in the area and were responsible for building the first dam across the river, as well as the first mill. By 1810, several more families had moved to Franklin, and the population reached 40 people. Christian Cackler married Theresa Nighman in 1814 at the town's first wedding. As the population continued to grow, two separate villages grew up in the township. The "Upper Village" was called Carthage, and the "Lower Village" was called Franklin Mills, though many people referred to them collectively as Franklin Mills, and as the two villages grew, they slowly merged into one larger village.

Planning for the Pennsylvania and Ohio Canal, which would go through Franklin Township, began in the 1820s. Investors, including Zenas Kent, moved to Franklin Mills and began buying property anticipating the boom that would undoubtedly follow the coming of the canal. The canal builders arrived sometime around 1836 and built a lock, a new dam, and a covered bridge. A business section grew in the town, and although the canal did benefit the people of Franklin Mills by providing a cheaper method of shipping, the big boom that was expected did not exactly occur, as the country was in a financial depression.

The Underground Railroad was active in Franklin Mills, and John Brown briefly called the village home in the 1830s. When the Civil War broke out, the Franklin Mills Rifle Company organized and joined the Company F of the Seventh Regiment, Ohio Volunteer Infantry. By the end of the Civil War, 161 men from Franklin Township had enlisted, and 135 came home.

9

Standing Rock has been a local landmark since before the first pioneers came to Kent. Located in the middle of the Cuyahoga River, a foot path crossed the river near here, and it has been said that local native tribes held their council meetings on top of this rock. Because of this, Standing Rock was also known as "Council Rock." (Courtesy of the Kent Historical Society.)

Settlers also used the foot path that passed by Standing Rock long after the natives had left the area. The size and prominence of the landmark inspired many people to take their pictures near or on the rock. (Courtesy of Kent State University Library Department of Special Collections and Archives.)

As the legend goes, Captain Samuel Brady and other army scouts were tracking a band of natives in 1780. The group was ambushed, and Brady managed to escape. The natives pursued him, and Brady eluded them by jumping over the Cuyahoga River and then hiding at what is now called Brady Lake. This is an early view of Brady's Leap, where people believe Captain Brady lept over the river. (Courtesy of the Kent Historical Society.)

In this later view from the late nineteenth century, Brady's Leap is seen where the river is at its narrowest. (Courtesy of John Carson.)

11

The Haymaker family was the first to settle in Franklin Township. They built the first dam and mill along the river, and when the mill proved unprofitable, they sold it and took up farming. This image from the 1874 Erie County Atlas shows the Haymaker farm. (Courtesy of the Kent Historical Society.)

Settlers from Ravenna and Hudson built the first Bridge in Franklin Township in 1803. In 1837, a new covered bridge was built at Main Street. After four decades of service, this covered bridge was replaced in 1877 with a stone bridge. (Courtesy of the Kent Historical Society.)

As more settlers came to the area, more businesses were established. Many of these new businesses were mills, including grist, saw, linseed oil, and woolen mills. Twin villages began to develop, though they were collectively called Franklin Mills, and that name stuck as the two villages slowly merged. The Kent Flour Mill, seen here, was built by Zenas Kent in the 1830s on the sight of the original Haymaker mill. (Courtesy of John Carson.)

The Mill Race for the Kent Flour Mill rerouted water from the river to power the mill, and then returned the water to the river. (Courtesy of John Carson.)

Zenas Kent moved to Ohio in 1812. In 1832, he purchased about 600 acres in Franklin Mills and began to develop numerous businesses, expecting them to grow and his property values to rise when the canal came through the village. (Courtesy of the Kent State University Department of Special Collections and Archives.)

One of the developments financed by Zenas Kent was the construction of the Kent Block, finished in 1837. Kent felt the village needed a business block and hotel, so he built them. The hotel and stores passed through numerous owners over the years. The hotel was first called the Franklin House. In 1872, it was renamed the Continental, and in 1889, it changed hands again and was renamed the Revere Hotel. (Courtesy of Kent Historical Society.)

Zenas Kent and his son Marvin, along with other investors, began work on a cotton mill in 1851. The five-story building was finished one year later, but it would remain empty until 1878 when Joseph Turner opened an Alpaca Mill there, with 52 looms in operation in the beginning. It remained one of the largest employers until the mills were moved to Cleveland in 1889. (Courtesy of the Kent Historical Society.)

Zenas Kent and John Brown went into partnership to build a tannery in 1835. Their partnership quickly dissolved, and Kent retained ownership of the tannery, seen here, which his son Marvin would manage for a number of years. Brown eventually left Franklin Mills, and in 1859, he led a raid at Harpers Ferry, West Virginia, and the rest is history. (Courtesy of Kent State University Library Department of Special Collections and Archives.)

15

A number of religious congregations organized in the early nineteenth century. The Methodists organized in 1815, the First Congregational Church organized in 1819, and the Episcopal Church organized in 1835. The Episcopal Church, seen here, was built in 1838. It was so well built that when the building was enlarged in 1900, they retained much of the original structure. (Courtesy of Kent State University Department of Special Collections and Archives.)

In 1827, the Church of Christ organized in Franklin Mills, and in 1848, the First Church of the Disciples of Christ reorganized. They began building a church in 1854, and the walls and roof were up by the following year when the congregation began to use the building. For financial reasons, the church would remain unfinished until 1868. (Courtesy of John Carson.)

The Pennsylvania and Ohio Canal, linking Pittsburgh and Cleveland, had been in the planning stages since 1827. Actual construction began in 1836, and the canal opened in 1840. The canal builders also rebuilt the dam that had been mostly washed away in 1832. The canal only had a two-decade life span, as the railroad soon put the canal out of business. (Courtesy of the Kent Historical Society.)

The Cuyahoga House was one of three early taverns in Franklin Mills. Before he became president, James Garfield stayed here at times when he drove mules for the canal. It was also rumored to be a stop on the Underground Railroad. In 1907, this house was torn down, and the columns were reused on a house in Ravenna. (Courtesy of Kent State University Library Department of Special Collections and Archives.)

Early pioneers were buried at a small cemetery on Stow Street, on land given by the Haymaker family. By the 1850s, there were no more lots available. At that point, the township purchased land on North Mantua Street near Standing Rock. They named the cemetery Standing Rock after the nearby landmark. Many people moved their families' remains to this new cemetery, and it became the main burial place for the township and village. The chapel was built in 1924. (Courtesy of John Carson.)

The Pioneer Association of Franklin Township met for the first time on October 20, 1874, at the home of Christian Cackler Sr. The following year, Marvin Kent took an interest in the group and provided land for future meetings, which became known as Pioneer Grounds. Pioneer Day became one of the largest celebrations in Kent over the following few decades, held until most of the early pioneers had passed away. (Courtesy of the Kent Historical Society.)

Two

THE VILLAGE OF KENT

The Atlantic and Great Western Railroad came to Franklin Mills in 1863, during the Civil War. Not only did the railroad run through the village, the railroad shops were also located here, bringing the boom to the area that people had hoped would come earlier with the canal. Marvin Kent had been influential in bringing the railroad and railroad shops to the area, and in 1864, a movement began to change the name of the village to Kent in his honor. The post office began using the name Kent that same year, though the name would not officially change until the village was incorporated in 1867. For the remainder of the nineteenth century, Kent would continue to grow.

With the population boom that came to Kent, there were a number of changes in the village. The first newspaper was issued in 1867. New schools and churches were built, as were new homes and businesses. Two other railroad companies laid tracks through Kent, and by the close of the nineteenth century, an interurban line also ran through Kent.

A number of civic improvements were also made. Plank sidewalks were built in 1868. Old bridges were replaced, and new bridges were built. In 1880, a wandering-cattle ordinance passed that said that any one allowing a cow, horse, or pig to wander through the streets of Kent could be arrested and fined. That same year, the wooden sidewalks were replaced with stone, brick, and gravel sidewalks, depending on where in Kent you lived. The village installed streetlights, first oil, then gas, and finally electric. In the 1890s, some of the major roads were graded, but the lesser-traveled roads remained in various states of disrepair until the new century.

Pioneer Day was first celebrated in 1873, and it became an annual event. The first band, the Kent Independent Band, was organized in Kent in 1883. Prohibition was an issue for Kent, and in 1889, the people voted to make the village "dry," although saloons did not actually close until 1908.

19

In 1863, Atlantic and Great Western Railroad laid tracks through Kent. Marvin Kent was one of the passengers on the first train that came through the village. When it was completed, the rail line stretched from New York to Dayton. In New York, the Atlantic and Great Western Railroad connected with the Erie Railroad line, and the rail line is often called the "Erie," as the Erie Railroad Company acquired the A&GW line in the 1890s. (Courtesy of the Kent Historical Society.)

Because of its location along the rail line, and Marvin Kent's influence, Kent was chosen as the site for the railroad shops. In 1864, construction began on the shops. The shops are seen here in 1868. (Courtesy of John Carson.)

Many people came into Kent, first to construct the railroad shops, then to work in those shops. Kent experienced a population growth, as almost 200 men came to the village to work, with many bringing their families. The photograph is of the Erie Railroad employees. (Courtesy of Kent State University Library Department of Special Collections and Archives.)

The railroad shops were originally built to repair locomotives, but by 1872, they began to repair freight and passenger cars instead. The railroad shops remained in business until 1930. (Courtesy of the Kent Historical Society.)

In 1874, the village began a movement to build a train depot. The depot opened to the public in June 1875 and contained telegraph and ticket offices, baggage rooms, and waiting rooms. (Courtesy of John Carson.)

The first floor of the depot also contained a kitchen and dining room, seen here. On the second floor, there were rooms for the restaurant proprietors. The second floor later housed the first reading room in Kent. (Courtesy of the Kent Historical Society.)

In the 1880s, two more rail lines came through Kent. One was the Connotton Valley Railroad that became the Wheeling and Lake Erie, and the other line was the Pittsburgh, Youngstown, and Chicago Railroad that eventually became the Baltimore and Ohio. (Courtesy of Kent State University Library Department of Special Collections and Archives.)

The Rivet Works was one of the railroad shops located in Kent. (Courtesy of John Carson.)

The space available at the railroad yards made them a good place for community gatherings, such as this July 4th celebration. (Courtesy of Kent State University Library Department of Special Collections and Archives.)

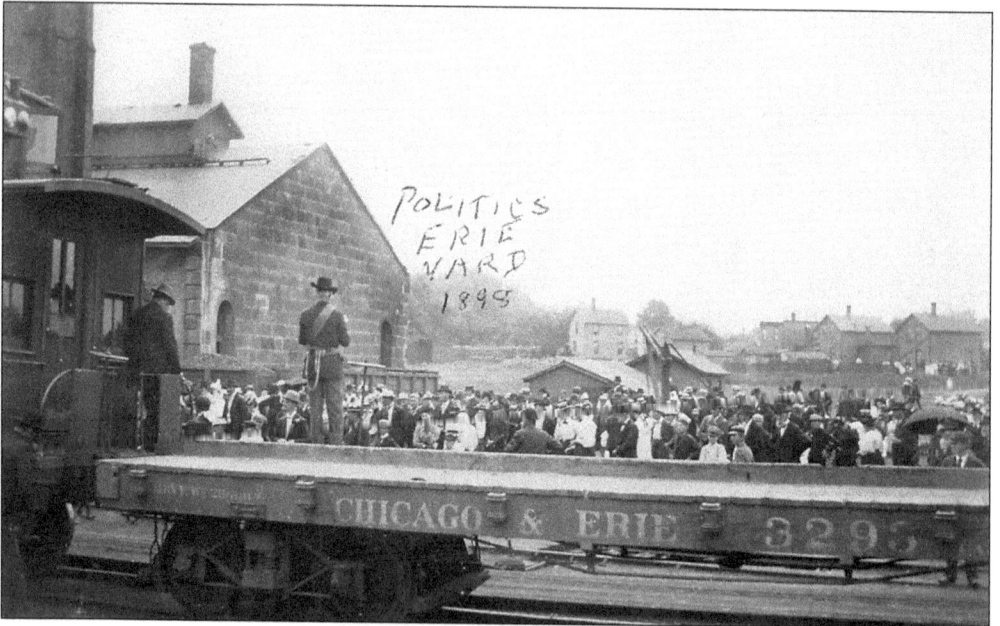

This image is simply labeled "Politics Erie Yard." Politicians would travel from one community to another by train, and people would gather to hear them speak. (Courtesy of Kent State University Library Department of Special Collections and Archives.)

A depot was built in 1882 for what would become the Wheeling and Lake Erie Railroad. Another depot for what would become the Baltimore and Ohio railroad was built in 1884, and rebuilt in 1905. The B&O depot is seen here. (Courtesy of John Carson.)

Three men are seen here unloading an Erie boxcar at the train depot. (Courtesy of John Carson.)

Marvin Kent, seen here seated and surrounded by his family, built a new home in 1880. Many skilled craftsmen were hired to finish the interior of his home, and it became a showplace. (Courtesy of Kent State University Library Department of Special Collections and Archives.)

After Marvin Kent's son, W.S. Kent, died in 1923, the Kent family sold the home to the Masons. The third floor became their lodge room. Recently, the Kent Homestead Preservation Association formed to raise money to preserve the building. (Courtesy of Kent State University Library Department of Special Collections and Archives.)

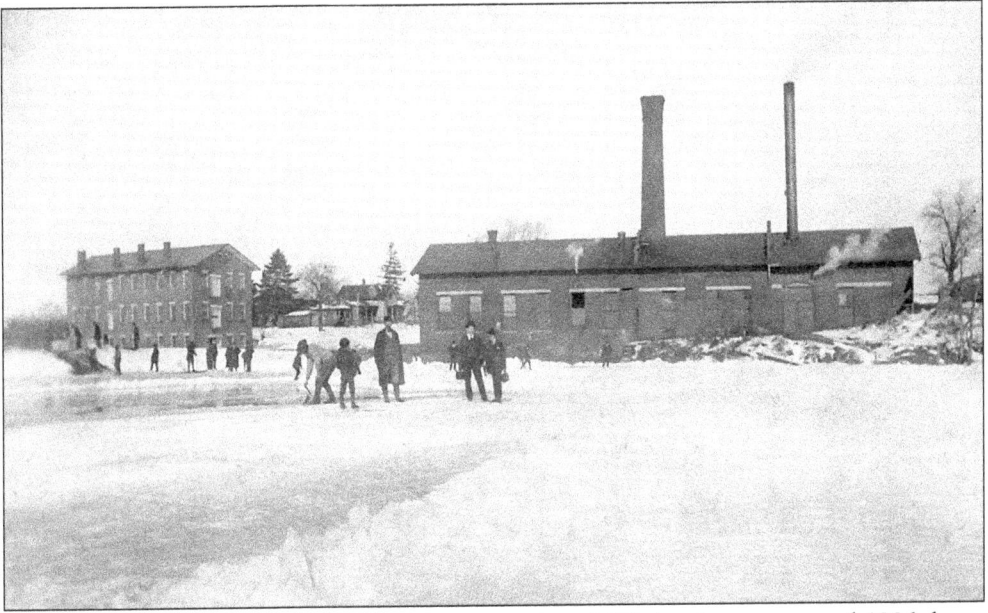

The need for a water works in Kent was seen as early as 1879, but it was not until 1886 that a vote to build a water works passed. When Plum Creek was selected as the site for the reservoir, it caused more opposition. But the work continued, and engines started pumping reservoir water into town in 1887. The water works building is the one on the right. (Courtesy of Kent State University Library Department of Special Collections and Archives.)

Well workers, such as those seen here, laid the pipes that extended water to all parts of the village. They also installed fire hydrants. (Courtesy of John Carson.)

In 1895, a 150-foot flag post was built at Depot Park, next to the train depot, just south of Main Street. A bell was placed in the tower, but people felt that the steel girders that surrounded it muted the sound. Still, the bell remained and was rung at celebrations. (Courtesy of Kent State University Library Department of Special Collections and Archives.)

The small park next to the train depot became a gathering point for many celebrations, such as the celebration of the end of the Spanish American War. (Courtesy of Kent State University Library Department of Special Collections and Archives.)

The water works company, in 1889, was given a five-year lighting contract. They were to build an electric light plant to provide and power electric lights on the streets of the village. The interior of that power plant is seen in this image. (Courtesy of Kent State University Library Department of Special Collections and Archives.)

The first telephone exchange was established in Kent in 1882. The service was not reliable, and lasted less than one year. Another company tried again in 1896, with more successful results. The Kent telephone operators from 1904 are seen here. (Courtesy of Kent State University Library Department of Special Collections and Archives.)

The tall post at the right side of the photograph is a weather signal tower. It was built in 1888 and stood 75 feet high. Each day, a signal was placed on the mast to show what type of weather was coming. (Courtesy of the Kent Historical Society.)

In 1895, an interurban line linked Akron and Kent. The line was intended to continue to Ravenna, but it was not completed until 1901. An interurban car can be seen here in the center of the image. Service was discontinued in 1932. (Courtesy of Kent State University Library Department of Special Collections and Archives.)

In 1870, the first Hook and Ladder Company was founded in Kent, and equipment and a firehouse were provided by the village. Following a fire in 1873, additional fire equipment was purchased, and three companies of volunteer fire fighters were organized. Hose Company Three is pictured here in 1887. (Courtesy of the Kent Historical Society.)

Those three fire companies still did not provide enough man power and equipment, as fires continued to be a challenge for the Village of Kent. The fire department remained a volunteer organization until 1923, when two full time firemen were employed by the city. (Courtesy of Kent State University Library Department of Special Collections and Archives.)

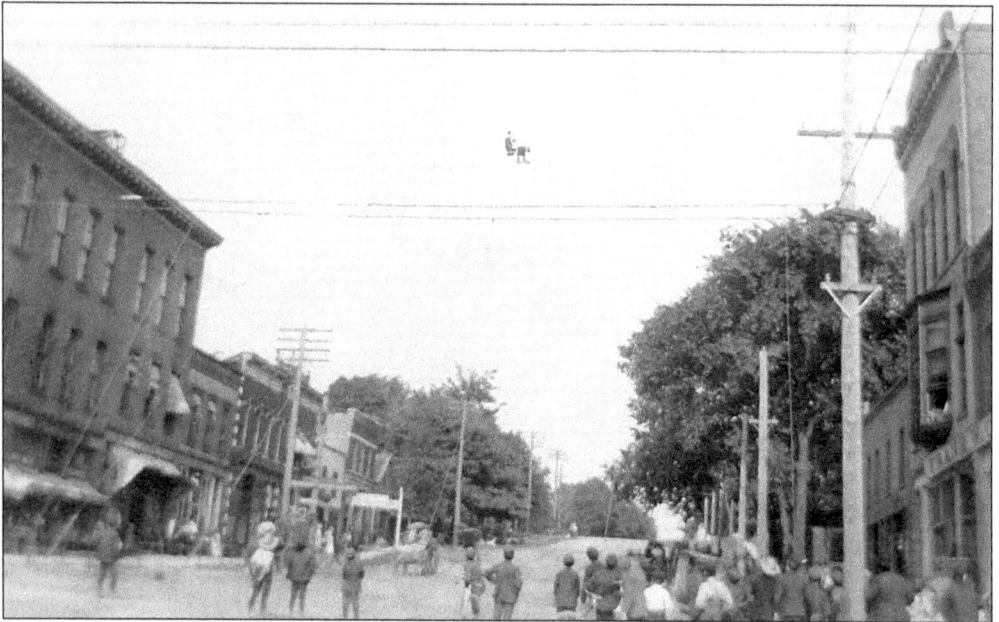

Though there is no identification on this image, it could very likely be Professor Leon (Jesse St. John), a famous tightrope walker. He came to Kent in 1874 and again in 1884, and each time, he walked a rope strung from the Alpaca Mill across the river to the glass works. He later married a girl from Kent. (Courtesy of Kent State University Library Department of Special Collections and Archives.)

The Frank W. Cone Dry Goods Store is seen here highly decorated, for an unidentified occasion. (Courtesy of Kent State University Library Department of Special Collections and Archives.)

On June 23, 1898, 14 men left Kent to join the Cleveland Grays, who were headed to serve in the Spanish American War. That group never saw action and returned to Kent in 1899. (Courtesy of Kent State University Library Department of Special Collections and Archives.)

Other young men joined the regular Army and did see action during the Spanish American War. When Santiago was captured in 1898, the community of Kent celebrated. (Courtesy of Kent State University Library Department of Special Collections and Archives.)

In 1877, a new suspension bridge was built, replacing an older wooden bridge. Two 100-foot iron cables were used in the construction of this bridge. (Courtesy of Kent State University Library Department of Special Collections and Archives.)

In 1876, the old covered bridge that crossed the Cuyahoga River at Main Street was replaced. Water was drained from the dam, and the first stone piers were laid before the old bridge was removed. (Courtesy of Kent State University Library Department of Special Collections and Archives.

The new Stone Arch Bridge was completed on September 22, 1877. The mayor placed the last keystone. The bridge was opened two days later. When completed, it was 60 feet wide and 275 feet long. (Courtesy of Kent State University Library Department of Special Collections and Archives.)

The Stone Arch Bridge is seen here with ice skaters on the river. A new park is currently being developed on this spot. (Courtesy of Kent State University Library Department of Special Collections and Archives.)

The Stow Street Bridge was built in 1897. Construction began in August and was finished by November. It is seen here while under construction, with the Kent Mill in the background. (Courtesy of Kent State University Library Department of Special Collections and Archives.)

The Stow Street Bridge is seen here after it was completed. (Courtesy of Kent State University Library Department of Special Collections and Archives.)

This view of Kent was taken sometime in the 1880s. The train depot is seen on the right, and the hill in the background is where Kent State University would eventually be built. (Courtesy of John Carson.)

This photograph provides a second view of Kent, taken by James Wark. Wark also took the other photograph on this page. (Courtesy of John Carson.)

John Davey, naturalist, author, and founder of the Davey Tree Expert Company, came to America in 1873. In the early 1880s, he moved to Kent and began working at Standing Rock Cemetery. He transformed the overgrown cemetery to a park-like setting. (Courtesy of Kent State University Library Department of Special Collections and Archives.)

John Davey began writing pamphlets and lecturing on natural subjects and developed a theory relating to the care of trees and of tree surgery. The Davey Family is seen here in front of their home, an ornate Gothic Revival structure. (Courtesy of Kent State University Library Department of Special Collections and Archives.)

John Davey became known around town as the "tree man." He and his eldest son planted hundreds of trees around the community, and people began to hire him to care for their trees. Some early Davey Tree Company employees are seen here with their tools. (Courtesy of Kent State University Library Department of Special Collections and Archives.)

In 1901, Davey published his book *The Tree Doctor*. He began to hire and train people to assist him with the workload, as he continued to write more articles about tree care. Employees are seen posing here with a tree they were working on. (Courtesy of Kent State University Library Department of Special Collections and Archives.)

Kent had been the site of two glass factories in its early history. Neither factory remained in business past 1837. In the 1850s, Kent, Wells & Co. established a new glass factory. In 1864, they sold it, and it was renamed Day, Williams & Co. Rock Glass Works. By 1870, they employed 100 people seasonally, but eventually went out of business in 1885. (Courtesy of the Kent Historical Society.)

In 1879, the Williams brothers established the Peerless Roller Mills to process flour. The growth of these mills put the old Kent Mill out of business, as it could not compete with the more modern methods that the Williams Brothers Mill used. (Courtesy of John Carson.)

The Kent National Bank Building was built at the corner of Main and Water Streets in 1867. Marvin Kent, Charles Kent, and the Kent National Bank Company paid for the construction of the building, with each owning various parts of the building. Marvin Kent opened an opera house on the top floor. (Courtesy of the Kent Historical Society.)

The interior of the Kent National Bank is seen here. The bank was located on the first floor of the building. (Courtesy of the Kent Historical Society.)

The exterior of J. Wark's Photograph Rooms on South Water Street is seen here. James Wark took the two photographs of Kent seen on page 37. (Courtesy of the Kent Historical Society.)

H. Stuckrad's Cigar Factory was located on South Water Street. The statue of an Indian and the posters in the windows were advertising gimmicks to draw people into the store. (Courtesy of John Carson.)

The stores of H.P. Dow, job printer, and N.H. Hall, coal dealer, were located on North Water Street. (Courtesy of Kent State University Library Department of Special Collections and Archives.)

Fred Bechtle's store was located on South Water Street. John Bechtle, Fred's father, came to Kent shortly after the Civil War. (Courtesy of the Kent Historical Society.)

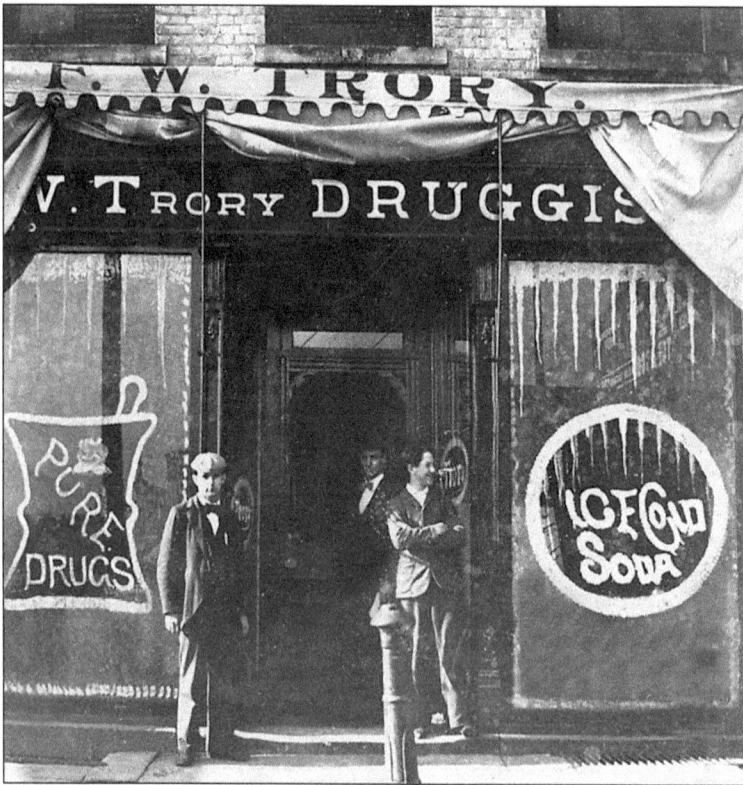

The Fred W. Trory Drugstore was located on Main Street. Fred was the brother of amateur photographer Art Trory, whose collection of photographs are housed at Kent State University. (Courtesy of Kent State University Library Department of Special Collections and Archives.)

The interior of the drug store is seen here c. 1917. (Courtesy of Kent State University Library Department of Special Collections and Archives.)

A new soda fountain was installed in Trory's Drugstore c. 1898. (Courtesy of Kent State University Library Department of Special Collections and Archives.)

Trory's served as a gathering place for some people, where they could go to share sodas and conversation. (Courtesy of Kent State University Library Department of Special Collections and Archives.)

Throughout the nineteenth century, horses were necessary for transportation. In 1870, five blacksmith shops were in operation in Kent. (Courtesy of the Kent Historical Society.)

Other businesses that assisted with horse-drawn transportation were the three livery stables, one feed store, one harness shop, and one wagon shop that were in business in Kent in 1870. The interior of the harness shop is seen here. (Courtesy of the Kent Historical Society.)

The Continental Hotel closed in 1889. It was then purchased by W.R. Carver, remodeled, and reopened as the Revere Hotel. (Courtesy of John Carson.)

The Wells Fargo Company was established in 1852, and some time prior to 1875, they opened an office in Kent. The Wells Fargo & Company Express Delivery Wagons are seen here from 1919. (Courtesy of the Kent Historical Society.)

In 1889, the International Order of Odd Fellows built an Opera House that included lodge rooms for their organization. Vaudeville companies held performances there, but the theater often had only small crowds. None of the theater's owners made much money in the venture. (Courtesy of John Carson.)

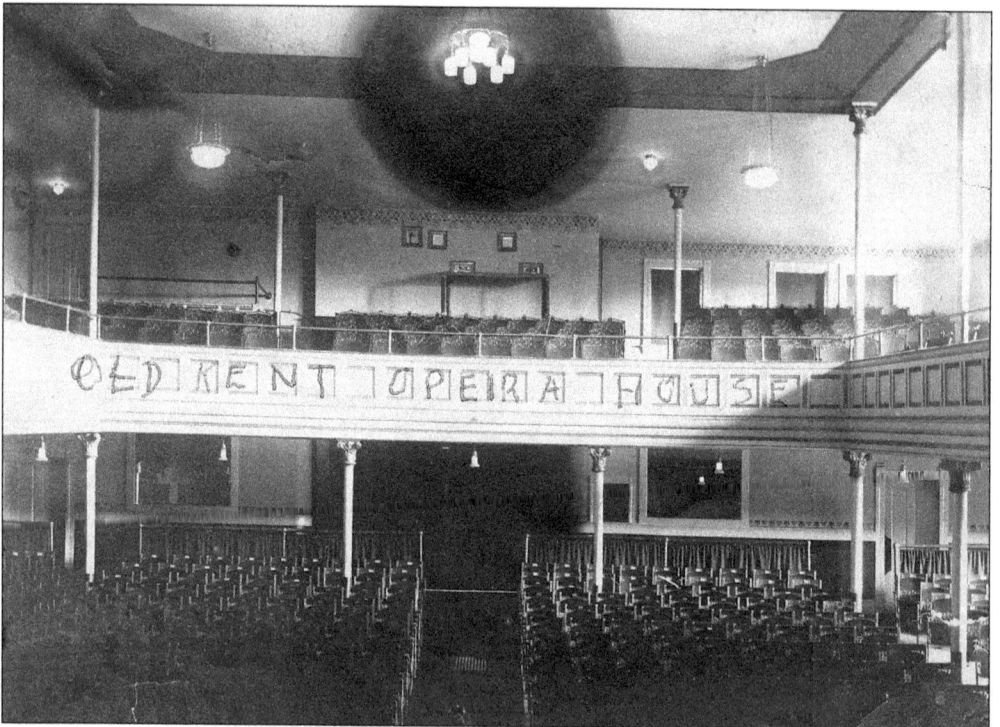

Shown here is the interior of the Opera House, looking towards the seats. (Courtesy of Kent State University Library Department of Special Collections and Archives.)

This view toward the stage of the Kent Opera House shows signs for a Howell Keith Company performance. (Courtesy of Kent State University Library Department of Special Collections and Archives.)

Two of the many performers who made appearances at the Kent Opera House were Count Magre and Mrs. Tom Thumb. (Courtesy of Kent State University Library Department of Special Collections and Archives.)

The shop of F.A. Coffeen, builder, is seen here. Small businesses were important to the growth of the Village of Kent. New buildings, both residential and commercial, were built by or with supplies from builders such as this one. (Courtesy of John Carson.)

Another small business was the shop of C.H. Woodard, tinner. (Courtesy of John Carson.)

A baseball team, the Kent Ball Club, was organized in Kent in the late 1890s. In 1900, that team won 27 of its 39 games. (Courtesy of Kent State University Library Department of Special Collections and Archives.)

In 1883, Alva Post formed the Kent Independent Band. The band lasted one year, and then Post left town. He came back to Kent in 1894 and founded the Post Band. This band continued until the Twin Coach Band was established in 1927. (Courtesy of the Kent Historical Society.)

In the 1890s, bicycling became both a popular sport and means of transportation. A speed limit was set within Kent at five miles per hour to prevent racing through the village. (Courtesy of the Kent Historical Society.)

Riverside Cycle Club met in a room at the Kent Opera House. In 1897, they sponsored a race from Kent to Aurora and back. (Courtesy of Kent State University Library Department of Special Collections and Archives.)

The first school in Kent was a one-room wooden structure built in 1817. Other school structures were built as needed, and the Union School System developed in 1860, which enabled the classes to be broken into grade levels. Union School was completed in 1869 and later was called Central School. (Courtesy of John Carson.)

A high school class was established in 1868, and when Union School was complete, the High School moved into that building. This is one of their graduating classes, c. 1882. Central School was rebuilt in 1954. (Courtesy of Kent State University Library Department of Special Collections and Archives.)

The population surge in Kent, brought on by the coming of the railroad shops, meant that Union School quickly ran out of space for students. A wood frame structure was built in 1869 to handle the overflow of students. In 1880, South School was built to replace the wooden structure. (Courtesy of John Carson.)

The interior of Dorthea Parsons' classroom at South School is seen here, c. 1916. South School later became known as Holden School. (Courtesy of the Kent Historical Society.)

In 1888, DePeyster School opened, again to handle the growing numbers of school age children in Kent. DePeyster cost $9,902 to build. (Courtesy of John Carson.)

In the mid-twentieth century, DePeyster briefly stood vacant. In the 1960s, the middle school needed more space, so the seventh-grade classes were moved to DePeyster. A fourth grade class from DePeyster School is seen here, from 1905. (Courtesy of Kent State University Library Department of Special Collections and Archives.)

The Methodists were founded in Kent in 1815. The first services were initially held at the homes of its members. Two years later, services moved to the combined church/schoolhouse and then to a new church building, both used by other sects as well. In 1840, the Methodists built a church solely for their use, seen here. (Courtesy of John Carson.)

By the 1880s, the Methodists began to plan for a new church building. In 1891, the cornerstone for the First Methodist Episcopal Church was placed. The building was completed two years later, at the cost of $21,500. (Courtesy of John Carson.)

The first Catholic mass held in Kent occurred around 1850. Plans for a Catholic church were begun in 1864, and it took three years to raise enough money to begin construction. St. Patrick's Church was completed one year later in 1868. (Courtesy of John Carson.)

The Congregational Church organized in Kent in 1819. This church was built in 1858 on the site of their earlier church building. The congregation purchased a bell for the bell tower in 1864, and they installed an organ in 1872. (Courtesy of John Carson.)

This view shows the Village of Kent on the west side of the Cuyahoga River just before the twentieth century. Central School, formerly Union School, is seen in the background. The Church of Christ is at the center, with St. Patrick's Catholic Church on the right. (Courtesy of John Carson.)

Three

NEARBY COMMUNITIES

The number of lakes in Franklin Township and near-by communities provided necessities like ice, as well as recreational opportunities. East Twin Lake and Brady Lake were both leased by ice companies at different times. They would harvest ice from the lakes in the winter months and store the ice until it was delivered to commercial and residential customers to use for refrigeration, until electrical refrigeration became the norm.

An amusement park developed at Silver Lake, called Randolph Park, and a second park developed at Brady Lake. The Brady Lake Park began with a dance pavilion and bathhouse in 1890 and developed into an amusement park with rides, including a roller coaster. In the 1940s, a nightclub and slot machines were added, and the gambling resort finally closed by 1950.

Parts of the history of Brimfield Township, located just south of Kent, are connected to the history of Kent. A number of Brimfield students attended high school at the Kent State Training School at Kent State University. Also through the years, there have been land debates between Brimfield and Kent, about whether certain parts of Brimfield should be annexed into Kent.

Because Ravenna was the County Seat, many people from Kent often had to travel to Ravenna to take care of business at the County Courthouse. In fact, Zenas Kent was the contractor who built the new courthouse building in Ravenna in 1830. Also, for a number of years in the nineteenth century, the Portage County Fair was held in Ravenna.

Located between Kent and Ravenna, Brady Lake first developed as a farming community. In 1890, A.G. Kent opened an amusement park at the lake. (Courtesy of Kent State University Library Department of Special Collections and Archives.)

A bathhouse, switch back railroad, and pony track were some of the attractions at the park. Two thousand people were on the park grounds for the grand opening. Cabins along the lakefront are seen here. (Courtesy of Kent State University Library Department of Special Collections and Archives.)

Among other attractions at the park, rowboats were available for rent, or you could take a ride on a 75-passenger steamer. After one season, the park was sold to an organization of Spiritualists, who continued to run the park for a number of years. (Courtesy of Kent State University Library Department of Special Collections and Archives.)

This photograph of Ida Kline was taken at Brady Lake. Numerous people and groups came to the lake for the amusements provided by the park. (Courtesy of Kent State University Library Department of Special Collections and Archives.)

The Spiritualists were not the only religious organization at Brady Lake. A Methodist Church was located in the village, and their Sunday School class is seen here. (Courtesy of Kent State University Library Department of Special Collections and Archives.)

The Brady Lake Hotel was built to house visitors who did not own cottages at the lake and was owned by the park. (Courtesy of the Kent Historical Society.)

A theater and dance pavilion were a central part of the park. Vaudeville performances and dance bands came through the area every summer. (Courtesy of Kent State University Library Department of Special Collections and Archives.)

In 1902, the park was sold and re-opened as Brady Lake Electric Park. The interurban line extended to the park, bringing more guests to the site. A roller coaster was added in the 1930s. The park finally closed in the early 1950s. (Courtesy of the Kent Historical Society.)

The park owned some of the cottages, like those seen in the background, while others were privately owned. Some lots were leased to people who then built cottages on their lots, and though they owned the cottages, they did not own the land, leading to unusual land tenure. (Courtesy of Kent State University Library Department of Special Collections and Archives.)

There were over 400 cottages at Brady Lake by 1916, including the Beckwith Cottage seen here. Before the dorms at Kent Normal School were completed, some of the first students stayed in these cottages. (Courtesy of Kent State University Library Department of Special Collections and Archives.)

Between the hotel, cottages, and campers, the summer population could reach almost 4,000 people in the summer season during Brady Lake's height of popularity. The Trory family, whose cottage is seen here, is one of those families who summered at Brady Lake. (Courtesy of Kent State University Library Department of Special Collections and Archives.)

Thanks to the many photographs taken by Art Trory, we have some images of cottage interiors, including this one of the porch of the Trory Cottage. (Courtesy of Kent State University Library Department of Special Collections and Archives.)

Ice harvesting occurred at Brady Lake from 1900 to 1924. Henry Spelman was the first to lease the lake for this purpose. At its busiest times, almost 200 men were hired to cut the ice, most of which were local farmers available to work during the winter months. (Courtesy of the Kent Historical Society.)

Some of the ice cut here was shipped as far as Cleveland and Youngstown by rail and was also used by the railroads in their refrigerator cars. (Courtesy of the Kent Historical Society.)

The ice house was built to store the cut ice until it was shipped. It had a storage capacity of 15,000 tons. (Courtesy of John Carson.)

On June 6, 1924, the ice house at Brady Lake caught fire, and that building was destroyed, along with 19 cottages. This event ended the ice harvesting at Brady Lake, which was already being affected by electrical refrigeration. (Courtesy of Kent State University Library Department of Special Collections and Archives.)

Randolph Park developed at Silver Lake. A theater opened in 1896, and the park became a popular destination. They had a merry-go-round, maze, and other amusement rides. The Pioneer Association held some of their earlier meetings here. (Courtesy of John Carson.)

These women were boating at Stewart Lake. Brady Lake was just one of many lakes in the areas surrounding Kent that provided weekend and summer amusement for those who lived nearby. (Courtesy of Kent State University Library Department of Special Collections and Archives.)

Another lake, Sandy Lake (Lake Stafford), was also a summer vacation spot. In 1877, the Cady family built a hotel. The hotel expanded in 1902 and again in 1918, but eventually business slowed down, and in the 1960s, the hotel was razed. The Kent State University Row Boat Regatta was formerly held on this lake. (Courtesy of Kent State University Library Department of Special Collections and Archives.)

Twin Lakes is the community just north of Kent. In 1882, the Forest City Ice Company leased East Twin Lake, seen here. They built an ice house on the south shore that could store 15,000 tons. (Courtesy of the Kent Historical Society.)

In 1922, the Twin Lakes Golf Club organized in 1922 as a social and recreational center for people in Kent and other communities. A clubhouse was built in 1926, and in 1932, the organization became the Twin Lakes Country Club. West Twin Lake is shown above. (Courtesy of the Kent Historical Society.)

Brimfield is the township just south of Kent. The Kelso House, shown here, was a community center in the nineteenth century. The Kelso family operated a tavern and an inn out of their home, where people headed to and from Kent could stop and have a meal or drink. Numerous community events were held here, including Christmas dances. The building is now the Kelso House Museum. (Courtesy of John Carson.)

Other community events for Brimfield Township occurred on the town square, which included the Town Hall and bandstand seen here. (Courtesy of the Brimfield Memorial House Association/Kelso House Museum.)

Numerous students from Brimfield completed their education in Kent. Brimfield High School had only a three-year program. Students could then go to Kent State High School to complete their fourth year of High School. (Courtesy of the Brimfield Memorial House Association/Kelso House Museum.)

The Portage County Courthouse was built in 1881, and as it was located in Ravenna. Numerous people from Kent often traveled to Ravenna for business and personal reasons. This building was the third County Courthouse; the first wood framed building was built in 1809, and the second was built in 1832 by Zenas Kent. This third courthouse was razed and replaced in 1960. (Courtesy of the Brimfield Memorial House Association/Kelso House Museum.)

Four

KENT IN THE
TWENTIETH CENTURY

Kent became a city in 1920. That year the population reached over 7,000 people. In the early years of the twentieth century, Kent saw some destructive fires and flooding. New businesses, such as the Twin Coach Company, opened, and old businesses, such as the Erie Railroad Shops, closed. The first automobile came to Kent, and the roads were paved, though parking and traffic would continue to be problems in Kent for decades to come. Kent State Normal School also opened in the early twentieth century and is discussed in Chapter 5. When World War I broke out, 726 men from Kent were registered for the draft.

In 1936, the Kent Community Chest and Welfare Association formed due to the high unemployment numbers that came with the closing of the railroad shops and other business that closed due to the aftermath of the stock market crash. The 1940s brought continued population growth and economic revival. With that growth, more residential houses were built on what used to be farmland, and new schools were needed. In the 1950s, two shopping plazas were built: the Stow-Kent Shopping Center and University Plaza, but the downtown businesses remained active.

Kent celebrated its sesquicentennial in 1956 with parades and pageants. In 1976, the city celebrated the bicentennial of the American Revolution, as did the rest of the country. In 1975, a city manager government replaced the position of mayor. The numbers of churches and social clubs grew, and the Kent Historical Society was founded in 1971. Shortly after their founding they bought and renovated the old railroad depot, where they operate a museum on the second floor.

As the twentieth century came to Kent, one of the more noticeable changes that occurred in the first decade was the growth in the number of automobiles. With that growth came more emphasis on street paving, parking, and traffic. The first traffic lights were located at the corners of Main and Water Streets and Crain and Mantua Streets. (Courtesy of Kent State University Library Department of Special Collections and Archives.)

The Kent Chamber of Commerce began as the Board of Trade, established in 1910. The name "Chamber of Commerce" was adopted in 1920. The Chamber's purpose is to promote Kent and advance economic growth. Members of the Chamber of Commerce are seen here on North Water Street in 1913, on their way to a ball game in Cleveland. (Courtesy of Kent State University Library Department of Special Collections and Archives.)

Throughout the nineteenth century, the post office was located wherever the current postmaster chose. In 1908, free mail delivery began, and in 1912, a new permanent post office was built on South Water Street, which was in use until a new post office was built in 1985. (Courtesy of John Carson.)

The first library in Kent was a reading room on the second floor of the train station. It then moved to various locations until Andrew Carnegie offered Kent $10,000 to build a library in 1901. The new library opened in 1903. (Courtesy of John Carson.)

On March 31, 1913, floods began in many parts of Ohio after a week of heavy rains. The river level rose above the level of the train tracks, holding train traffic up for days. Also, homes and businesses near the river flooded. (Courtesy of John Carson.)

The 1913 Flood also destroyed the old canal lock and did a great deal of damage to the dam. The dam was not repaired until 1925, after a debate over whether it should be removed, as it was no longer functional. (Courtesy of John Carson.)

On November 8 and 9, 1913, Kent received two feet of snow in two days time. Transportation stopped, as roads were impassable and interurbans were snowed in. (Courtesy of John Carson.)

People were stranded in stores and homes until they were able to shovel out after the snow stopped falling. (Courtesy of John Carson.)

On February 12, 1912, the Longcoy Building caught fire. Firemen were quickly on the scene, but the building was destroyed. Both the Thompson and France Buildings, next to the Longcoy Building, were also heavily damaged. (Courtesy of Kent State University Library Department of Special Collections and Archives.)

When World War I began in 1917, 23 men from Kent enlisted in the Ohio National Guard within two weeks. The first soldiers from Portage County, some of which were probably men from Kent, are seen here on the steps of the Portage County Courthouse. (Courtesy of the Kent Historical Society.)

The women of Kent did their part during the war by joining and supporting the Red Cross. The directors of the Portage County Chapter of the American Red Cross are seen here at the home of Mrs. W.S. Kent on June 10, 1919. (Courtesy of Kent State University Library Department of Special Collections and Archives.)

When news of the end of the war reached Kent on November 11, 1918, the town celebrated. An impromptu parade began, with people marching through town, with the mayor and others addressing the gathering crowds. (Courtesy of Kent State University Library Department of Special Collections and Archives.)

In 1911, Calbraith Perry Rodgers made the first transcontinental flight in a Wright brothers' biplane. He landed about 70 times between New York and California, and one of those stops was just outside of Kent, where amateur photographer Arthur Trory took this photograph. (Courtesy of Kent State University Library Department of Special Collections and Archives.)

Martin Davey, son of John Davey (founder of the Davey Tree Company), became Ohio's 53rd governor in 1935. He was born and raised in Kent and served two terms as governor. He is seen here with an unknown pilot. (Courtesy of Kent State University Library Department of Special Collections and Archives.)

The Sanitary Ice Company formed in 1915. They built the first ice plant in Portage County and made their early deliveries with two Ford trucks. (Courtesy of Kent State University Library Department of Special Collections and Archives.)

In 1915, the Mason Tire and Rubber Company organized. They built a plant one year later, and the company prospered until the 1921 financial panic. By 1929, financial problems caught up with the company, and the factory was sold. The company closed the next year. Leroy Kline is the truck driver seen in the photograph. (Courtesy of John Carson.)

In the early 1890s, there was some concern that Kent had stopped growing. Not enough new businesses were moving to the area. The town offered to build a new factory as an incentive to bring a new company to the area that would employ at around 300 people. The factory was built, but the company backed out of the agreement. In 1897, the company of Kearny & Foote purchased the factory. (Courtesy of Kent State University Library Department of Special Collections and Archives.)

Kearney & Foote employed nearly 200 people by 1899. In 1901, Kearney & Foote was sold to a company from Rhode Island, and the factory was closed. (Courtesy of Kent State University Library Department of Special Collections and Archives.)

Charles Gougler established the Gougler Machine Company in 1921 with only four machine tools. The company slowly grew, with business picking up after they began making tools for the Davey Tree Company. Company employees are seen here outside the machine shop. (Courtesy of the Kent Historical Society.)

In 1926, the Lamson-Sessions Company absorbed the Falls Rivet Company, which occupied the Kearney & Foote Factory after Kearney & Foote closed. Lamson-Sessions grew over the years and expanded their facilities in the 1970s, before it was sold to Russell, Burdsall, and Ward Corporation. (Courtesy of Kent State University Library Department of Special Collections and Archives.)

The Seneca Chain Company was incorporated in 1900 as the Kent Chain Company, which then merged with the Seneca Manufacturing Company to create the Seneca Chain Company. By 1909, over 400 people were employed by the company to manufacture chains. (Courtesy of John Carson.)

The interior of the Seneca Chain Company is seen here, with piles of chains on the floor. In December of 1909, a fire spread throughout the factory, destroying everything. They rebuilt the factory, but financial troubles caused them to close shortly thereafter. (Courtesy of John Carson.)

The Fageol Brothers founded the Twin Coach Company in 1927. The company designed and manufactured many types of vehicles, though their most successful line was their line of buses. Twin Coach buses were used in cities across the country, and they were the first to use a diesel engine. (Courtesy of the Kent Historical Society.)

The factory interior is seen here. During World War II, the company produced items that aided the war effort, including tail assemblies for planes and control cabins for blimps. After the war, production returned to buses. By 1948, bus sales had declined, and in 1953, bus production stopped at the Kent factory. (Courtesy of the Kent Historical Society.)

A military contract briefly revived production at the Kent plant in the 1950s. The factory was then used to refit buses with new engines and briefly used to produce mail delivery trucks. In the 1960s, production at the factory ceased for good. The photograph here was taken on Twin Coach Day, August 15, 1937. (Courtesy of the Kent Historical Society.)

Some of the Twin Coach Company employees are seen here at this diner for their fieldmen and formen, held at the Twin Lakes Country Club on June 19, 1945. (Courtesy of Kent State University Library Department of Special Collections and Archives.)

Some Twin Coach Company employees were very active in the community. The Twin Coach Band was formed in 1927 by the employees. They are seen here giving a benefit concert at Roosevelt High School, December 19, 1935. (Courtesy of the Kent Historical Society.)

Twin Coach employees also formed a baseball team that competed against other local teams. (Courtesy of the Kent Historical Society.)

In 1909, the Davey Institute of Tree Surgery was established to train people to perform tree surgery. Early classes met in Kent Hall, above Kent National Bank. (Courtesy of Kent State University Library Department of Special Collections and Archives.)

Enrollment in the school grew each year, and men are seen here practicing the techniques they would have learned in class. (Courtesy of Kent State University Library Department of Special Collections and Archives.)

In 1909, John Davey, with his son Martin, officially incorporated the business as the Davey Tree Expert Company. By 1929, the company had 1,000 trained employees in the field. The office staff is seen here, from the 1920s. (Courtesy of Kent State University Library Department of Special Collections and Archives.)

More Davey Tree Company employees can be seen here in this image of a company banquet. The Davey Tree Expert Company remains one of Kent's largest and longest operating businesses. (Courtesy of Kent State University Library Department of Special Collections and Archives.)

Charles Sawyer and Milton Kneifel established a grocery store in Kent. In 1905, Burt Kneifel, Milton's brother, bought out Sawyer, and the company became Kneifel Grocery Company. (Courtesy of the Kent Historical Society.)

Kneifel Grocery Company used this truck for deliveries. Kenneth Nash is the driver. (Courtesy of the Kent Historical Society.)

W.L. Fox Co. Groceries used this delivery wagon, *c.*1908. (Courtesy of the Kent Historical Society.)

Emmet Kline established a grocery store in Kent in 1910. It was one of 11 grocery stores in Kent at the time and managed to be one of the longest lasting, finally closing in 1989. (Courtesy of the Kent Historical Society.)

Arthur Trory opened a bakery next door to the F.W. Trory Drug Store in 1900. Their two delivery wagons are pictured in front of the store entrance. (Courtesy of Kent State University Library Department of Special Collections and Archives.)

The interior of Trory's bakery is shown here. Arthur Trory was also an amateur photographer, taking many of the photographs in this book. (Courtesy of Kent State University Library Department of Special Collections and Archives.)

The Philfules Company provided natural gas to homes in Kent. (Courtesy of Kent State University Library Department of Special Collections and Archives.)

The interior of the W.H. Donaghy Drug Company is seen here from the early 1900s. (Courtesy of Kent State University Library Department of Special Collections and Archives.)

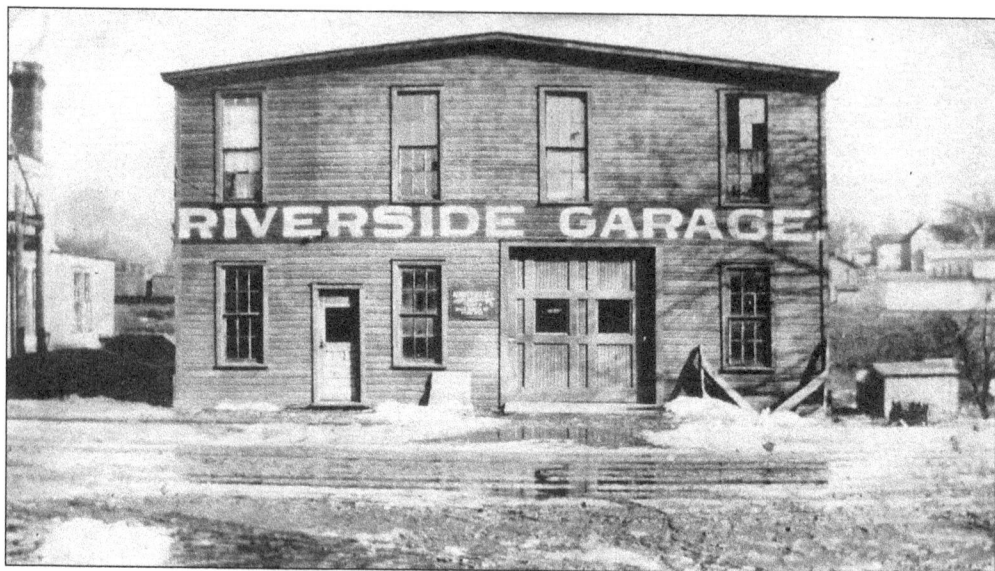

The first automobile came to Kent in 1901. As the automobile became a more popular mode of transportation, repair shops became more numerous, including Riverside Garage, seen here. (Courtesy of the Kent Historical Society.)

Fred Haymaker, a descendent of the first settlers to arrive in Franklin Township, opened a Ford agency in Kent in 1915 and built a garage for repairs that same year. The garage interior is seen here. (Courtesy of the Kent Historical Society.)

This photograph of Water Street was possibly taken in the early 1930s. The Kent Opera House is still standing on the right, and the interurban tracks can still be seen in the center of the road. (Courtesy of the Kent Historical Society.)

In 1964, the Opera House was demolished. Originally a vaudeville theater, it was converted to a movie theater, but always suffered from financial problems. (Courtesy of the Kent Historical Society.)

Roosevelt High School was built in 1922 to house grades 9 through 12. In 1959, a new high school was built and the old high school became Davey Junior High School. (Courtesy of the Kent Historical Society.)

The staff of Roosevelt High School is seen here in this image from 1937. (Courtesy of the Kent Historical Society.)

The 1931 Roosevelt High School Football Team is seen here. In 1922, the high school team won the Trolley League (Western Reserve League) Championship. (Courtesy of the Kent Historical Society.)

There was a second high school in Kent, located at Kent State University, which enrolled students from Franklin and Brimfield Townships, outside of the city limits of Kent. Howard Johnson played on the Kent State High School basketball team, which won the Class B state championship in 1927. (Courtesy of John Carson.)

The group above gathered for the laying of the cornerstone for Trinity Lutheran Church on August 15, 1908. At that time, the Church was still known as the First Evangelical Lutheran Church, founded in 1877. This building replaced their first wooden church built in 1884. (Courtesy of Kent State University Library Department of Special Collections and Archives.)

The original wooden Lutheran church structure was moved to the rear of the lot, and this new stone church was dedicated on February 28, 1909. The Lutheran congregation in 1920 adopted the name Trinity Evangelical Lutheran Church. (Courtesy of John Carson.)

In early 1921, a charter was granted for Portage Post No. 496 of the American Legion. By May, their membership had reached almost 200 people. They acquired an old Kent family home on South River Street in 1923 for their first headquarters. (Courtesy of John Carson.)

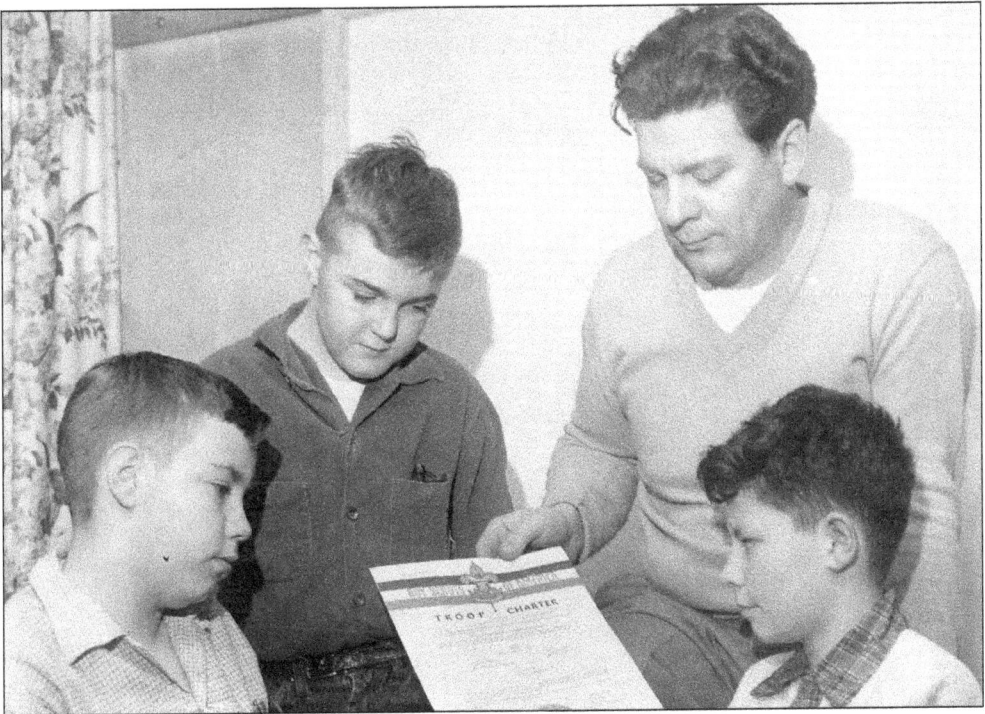

The first recorded Boy Scout troop in Kent, led by Reverend John H. Hull, organized in 1915 and met at the Congregational Church. The first Girl Scout troop, led by Katherine R. McArthur, organized in 1926, and also met at the Congregational Church. Here, we see a later Boy Scout troop with their charter. (Courtesy of Kent State University Library Department of Special Collections and Archives.)

Kent held its sesquicentennial in 1956. A parade ran through the city and a pageant was held on the Kent State University campus. (Courtesy of the Kent Historical Society.)

Like many other communities across America, Kent joined the celebration of the bicentennial of the American Revolution in 1976. Numerous events and activities were held between April 1975 and July 1976, culminating in a daylong festival. Events that day included a bus tour of historic Kent, on the tour bus seen here, concerts, symposium, and publications. (Courtesy of the Kent State University Library Department of Special Collections and Archives.)

Five

KENT STATE UNIVERSITY

Ohio had only three schools at the beginning of the twentieth century that provided preparation for teachers, all of which were located in the southern half of the state In 1910, the Lowry Bill passed, which would create two new normal schools: one in the northeast and one in the northwest parts of Ohio. Almost 40 communities applied, and in November 1910, Kent was chosen as the site for the Northeast Ohio normal school, in part due to William S. Kent's gift of the 53-acre Kent farm, while Bowling Green was chosen as the northwest normal school. The northeast school would be named Kent State in honor of William S. Kent's land donation. Edwin F. Moulton became the chairman of the Board of Trustees, appointed in July 1911. John McGilvery served as the first president, and George Hammond was selected to design the new campus. In May of 1913, the first summer session on campus began. Classes were held in Merrill Hall, and Lowry Hall served as the first Dormitory. September 1913 began the first full academic year, with 144 students enrolled. That first summer three new buildings were planned: Kent Hall, the Administration Building, and a power plant. Enrollment numbers were higher than anticipated, and by the Spring Semester of 1914, there were over 1600 students. Spring of 1913 also saw the first Campus Day tradition.

As the enrollment numbers continued to grow, so did the number of buildings on campus. Moulton Hall was built in 1917, Wills Gymnasium in 1924, Franklin Hall (originally called the Training School) in 1926, and Rockwell Hall became the library in 1928. A college of liberal arts was established at Kent in 1929, and four-year baccalaureate degrees were granted, as Kent State Normal College became Kent State College. A school of business administration followed in 1935, and a graduate program also began, giving university status to Kent State.

The lack of jobs during the Depression sent many people back to school, so enrollment numbers did not drop. World War I sent many men overseas, and the numbers of women on campus outnumbered the men. In the 1940s and 50s, more new buildings were constructed, including McGilvery Hall, which was built as a WPA Project in 1939. These new buildings began the spread of the campus to the southeast.

The 1960s saw another building boom. The numbers of classroom buildings and residence halls increased, and in 1970, the new library was complete. As well as the number of buildings, the number of master's degrees also increased, and the first doctoral programs began.

Many people associate the date May 4, 1970, with Kent State. The tragic events that occurred on campus that day, which ended with the death of four people, are remembered each year with a memorial. Kent State University was able to recover from that tragedy, and it has continued to grow and thrive to the present day.

In 1910, William Kent, son of Marvin Kent, offered his 53-acre farm for the state to build a normal school, or teachers training college, in Northeast Ohio. The site became known as Normal Hill, on the left side of the image, before the construction of any campus buildings had begun. (Courtesy of John Carson.)

John Edward McGilvrey, the first president of the school, began extension classes in 25 communities in Northeast Ohio. Construction of the new campus buildings were underway, but McGilvrey was anxious to begin classes, and over 1,000 students were enrolled at these extension sites. These classes were held in the fall of 1912 and spring of 1913. (Courtesy of Kent State University Library Department of Special Collections and Archives.)

George F. Hammond, an architect from Cleveland, designed the initial campus buildings with their classical facades. He and McGilvrey chose to lay out the new buildings in a semicircle along the top of the hill. (Courtesy of John Carson.)

On June 18, 1912, there was a ceremony for the laying of the cornerstone of Merrill Hall. Named for Frank A. Merrill, this first classroom building also housed administrative offices and the library. (Courtesy of Kent State University Library Department of Special Collections and Archives.)

Lowry Hall, named for John Hamilton Lowry, was built in 1913 as the first dormitory for women. From the start, one dormitory was not enough to house all the students. Homeowners from Kent, Brady Lake, Ravenna, Twin Lakes, and other near-by communities provided rooms for male students and female students who could not fit in the dorms. (Courtesy of John Carson.)

The first dining hall was located in Lowry Hall, seen here. A new, more stylish, dining hall was added to Lowry Hall in the mid-1920s. (Courtesy of Kent State University Library Department of Special Collections and Archives.)

The first summer term began on May 19, 1913, with only 47 students. The second summer term began on June 16, and the enrollment numbers were up to 290 students. Thirty-four students made up the first graduating class of 1914. Those early students are seen here, in front of Merrill Hall, with Lowry Hall seen in the back. (Courtesy of Kent State University Library Department of Special Collections and Archives.)

The quick growth of the school encouraged the state to construct three more buildings: an administration building, a power plant, and a second classroom building, Kent Hall. Though the postcard refers to this building as the administration building, it is Merrill Hall. (Courtesy of John Carson.)

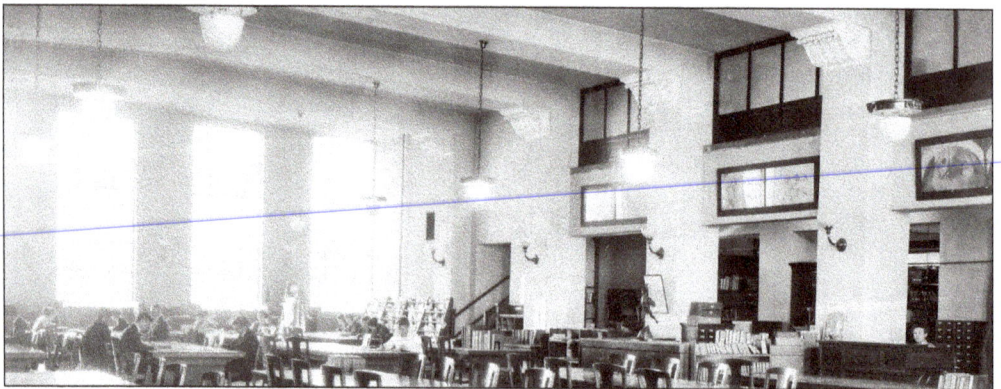

The library moved from Merrill Hall to the first floor atrium of the new administration building in 1915. (Courtesy of Kent State University Library Department of Special Collections and Archives.)

This image shows the front campus in 1915. Kent Hall, known briefly as the Science Hall, is on the right, with the unfinished Administration Building to its left, then Merrill Hall. (Courtesy of Kent State University Library Department of Special Collections and Archives.)

The Administration Building, known today as the Auditorium, housed presidential and other administrative offices, and at different times, a library, a health center, the registrar, the bursar, and other departments as needed. (Courtesy of John Carson.)

The continued increase in enrollment necessitated even more new buildings. Moulton Hall was built in 1917 as the second dorm for women. (Courtesy of John Carson.)

An interior view of a dorm room at Mouton Hall is seen here. In the early 1960s, when overcrowding in the dorms was at a high, some female students were housed in the basement halls of Moulton. (Courtesy of Kent State University Library Department of Special Collections and Archives.)

The first commencement was held on July 29, 1914. Thirty-four students, who had begun their coursework at some of the many satellite campuses before the buildings on the main campus were complete, received a two-year diploma. The ceremony was held in the Tabernacle, a temporary wooden structure located on the lawns of Front Campus. (Courtesy of Kent State University Library Department of Special Collections and Archives.)

Later commencement ceremonies were held in the Auditorium in the Administration Building, and then the Memorial Gym. (Courtesy of Kent State University Library Department of Special Collections and Archives.)

This aerial view of the campus was taken around 1918. Moulton Hall is to the far left. (Courtesy of John Carson.)

Prentice Gate was the main entrance to the front campus, at the corner of East Main and Lincoln Streets. (Courtesy of John Carson.)

Rockwell Hall was built in 1928 as the first library building on campus. An addition was added in 1958 and housed executive offices before becoming the home of the School of Fashion Design and Merchandising in 1989. The original part of the building houses the Kent State University Museum. (Courtesy of John Carson.)

When Rockwell Hall was completed, the library moved there from the atrium of the Administration Building. Rockwell remained the library building until the current library opened in 1970. (Courtesy of Kent State University Library Department of Special Collections and Archives.)

As Kent was a teacher training college originally, students were given the opportunity to observe other teachers at work. Some of those students are seen here observing a class through the windows. (Courtesy of Kent State University Library Department of Special Collections and Archives.)

An early art class is seen in this photograph. (Courtesy of Kent State University Library Department of Special Collections and Archives.)

112

Kent Hall was first built as the science building. A chemistry classroom is seen here. (Courtesy of Kent State University Library Department of Special Collections and Archives.)

A harness-making class is in process in this photograph. Besides offering teachers training courses, Kent offered classes in the industrial arts. (Courtesy of Kent State University Library Department of Special Collections and Archives.)

Kent State Normal College had its first baseball team in 1914. School custodian Alex Whyte founded and coached the team until 1927. This team photograph was taken *c.* 1920. (Courtesy of Kent State University Library Department of Special Collections and Archives.)

Paul Chandler, a professor in the Department of Education, coached the first football team in 1922. (Courtesy of the Kent Historical Society.)

Kent State Training School provided elementary and high school classes for students from Kent and other near-by communities. They had their own sports teams, including this men's basketball team from 1926. In 1927, they won the Class B State Championship. (Courtesy of the Kent Historical Society.)

Though this photograph is of the high school team, Kent State had their first women's basketball team in 1917. (Courtesy of Kent State University Library Department of Special Collections and Archives.)

Music has been just as important to student life as sports. The Concert Band was one option available to students who played an instrument. (Courtesy of Kent State University Library Department of Special Collections and Archives.)

The Symphony Orchestra was another group students who played an instrument could audition for. (Courtesy of Kent State University Library Department of Special Collections and Archives.)

For those who preferred singing, they could audition for the Mixed Chorus. (Courtesy of Kent State University Library Department of Special Collections and Archives.)

The College Band played at university events and sports games. (Courtesy of Kent State University Library Department of Special Collections and Archives.)

The first Campus Day celebration was held in 1914. There were speeches, singing, and dancing around the maypole. (Courtesy of Kent State University Library Department of Special Collections and Archives.)

The maypole dance tradition was still held into the 1930s, seen here on front campus, in front of the auditorium. (Courtesy of Kent State University Library Department of Special Collections and Archives.)

Wills Gymnasium was built in 1924, attached to the administration building and built over what was once Blackbird Lake. The interior is seen here, with a gym class from 1934 in session. (Courtesy of Kent State University Library Department of Special Collections and Archives.)

The Wills Gym was the only gym on campus until 1950, when the Memorial Gymnasium opened. They still used Wills Gym, for classes such as the dance class seen above, and for student registration. In the 1960s, when housing was again a problem, Wills Gym even briefly served as a men's dormitory. (Courtesy of Kent State University Library Department of Special Collections and Archives.)

On-campus housing, or lack thereof, has been a problem at Kent State from the beginning. These women holding a banner saying "Normal Inn" are more than likely students who could not find on-campus housing and ended up living together at a place they dubbed "Normal Inn."(Courtesy of Kent State University Library Department of Special Collections and Archives.)

In 1960, Kent State University celebrated its semicentennial. Paul J. Baus, then an associate professor in the School of Art, created the design for the semicentennial sign. (Courtesy of Kent State University Library Department of Special Collections and Archives.)

Homecoming Queen Nelda Norton, Ray Mantle, University President George Bowman, Alumni Association President Jack Harris, and Student Council President William Lahl are seen here at the Semicentennial Homecoming. (Courtesy of Kent State University Library Department of Special Collections and Archives.)

On May 1, 1970, student demonstrations began in response to the invasion of Cambodia. They were held both on campus and in the City of Kent. That evening, the crowd broke many business windows during demonstrations. The next evening, May 2nd, demonstrators set fire to the ROTC building on campus. National Guard Troops were brought in to maintain order. (Courtesy of Kent State University Library Department of Special Collections and Archives.)

On May 3rd, the National Guard blocked most campus entrances. Faculty senators circulated among students, urging them to stay calm and not attempt any further disturbances. Students are seen here on May 4, in the area known as the Commons. (Courtesy of Kent State University Library Department of Special Collections and Archives.)

That evening, May 3rd, students gathered around the Victory Bell. When they ignored an order to leave, the National Guard fired tear gas at them, which pushed them off campus. Students are seen here at the Victory Bell again on May 4th. (Courtesy of Kent State University Library Department of Special Collections and Archives.)

On May 4th, students again gathered at the Commons. Some of those students are seen here in front of Taylor Hall. (Courtesy of Kent State University Library Department of Special Collections and Archives.)

The National Guard was brought in to remove students and demonstrators from the Commons. They fired tear gas into the crowds to attempt to disperse them. Empty canisters were then thrown back at the troops, at which point the troops opened fire. (Courtesy of Kent State University Library Department of Special Collections and Archives.)

After 13 seconds of gunfire, four people were dead: Allison Krause, Jeffrey Miller, Sandra Scheuer, and William Schroeder. Nine others were wounded that day. With faculty intervention, students and other demonstrators disbursed, and the campus was closed. (Courtesy of Kent State University Library Department of Special Collections and Archives.)

At a candlelight memorial service, Dean Kahler, one of nine students injured on May 4th, is seen holding a candle where Jeffrey Miller died. (Courtesy of Kent State University Library Department of Special Collections and Archives.)

The events of May 4, 1970, are remembered each year. There have been candlelight memorial services, such as the one seen here in 1975, as well as symposiums on peace and democracy. (Courtesy of Kent State University Library Department of Special Collections and Archives.)

In January 1970, artist Robert Smithson came to Kent State and created his site-specific work *Partially Buried Woodshed*, at the corner of Summit Street and Rhodes Road. He did this by taking 20 truckloads of earth and an abandoned shed, and using bulldozers, he piled the earth against the shed. (Courtesy of Kent State University Library Department of Special Collections and Archives.)

Shortly after the events of May 4th, "May 4 Kent" was painted on the shed, and the work took on a new meaning—one of remembrance. In 1975, part of the shed was burned, and in 1984, the remainder of the structure was removed from campus. (Courtesy of Kent State University Library Department of Special Collections and Archives.)

Today's campus center, seen here in the 1970s, includes the library and student center. The library, the 12-story building in the center, was built in 1970, and the Student Center, to the left of the library, was completed shortly after. (Courtesy of Kent State University Library Department of Special Collections and Archives.)

A common sight today at Kent State University, black squirrels were first brought to the campus in 1961. Larry Woodell and M.W. Staples brought 10 black squirrels down from Canada, and their numbers have been growing ever since. (Courtesy of Kent State University Library Department of Special Collections and Archives.)

FURTHER READING

Caccamo, James F. *The Story of Kent, Ohio*. Kent, Ohio: The Kent Historical Society, 1999.

Darrow, Ralph, ed. *Kent, Ohio: The Dynamic Decades, A History of the Community from the 1930's to the 1990's*. Kent, Ohio: The Kent Historical Society, 1999.

Grismer, Karl H. *The History of Kent: Historical and Biographical*. Kent, Ohio: The Courier-Tribune, 1932.

Havran, Kenneth John. "The Village of Brady Lake, Ohio, 1900–1970: A Study of the Change in Function of a Northeastern Ohio Community." Masters Thesis, Kent State University, 1973.

Hildebrand, William H., Dean H. Keller, and Anita D. Herington. *A Book of Memories: Kent State University, 1910–1992*. Kent, Ohio: The Kent State University Press, 1993.

Troyer, Loris C. *Portage Pathways*. Kent, Ohio: The Kent State University Press, 1998.

Visit us at
arcadiapublishing.com

···

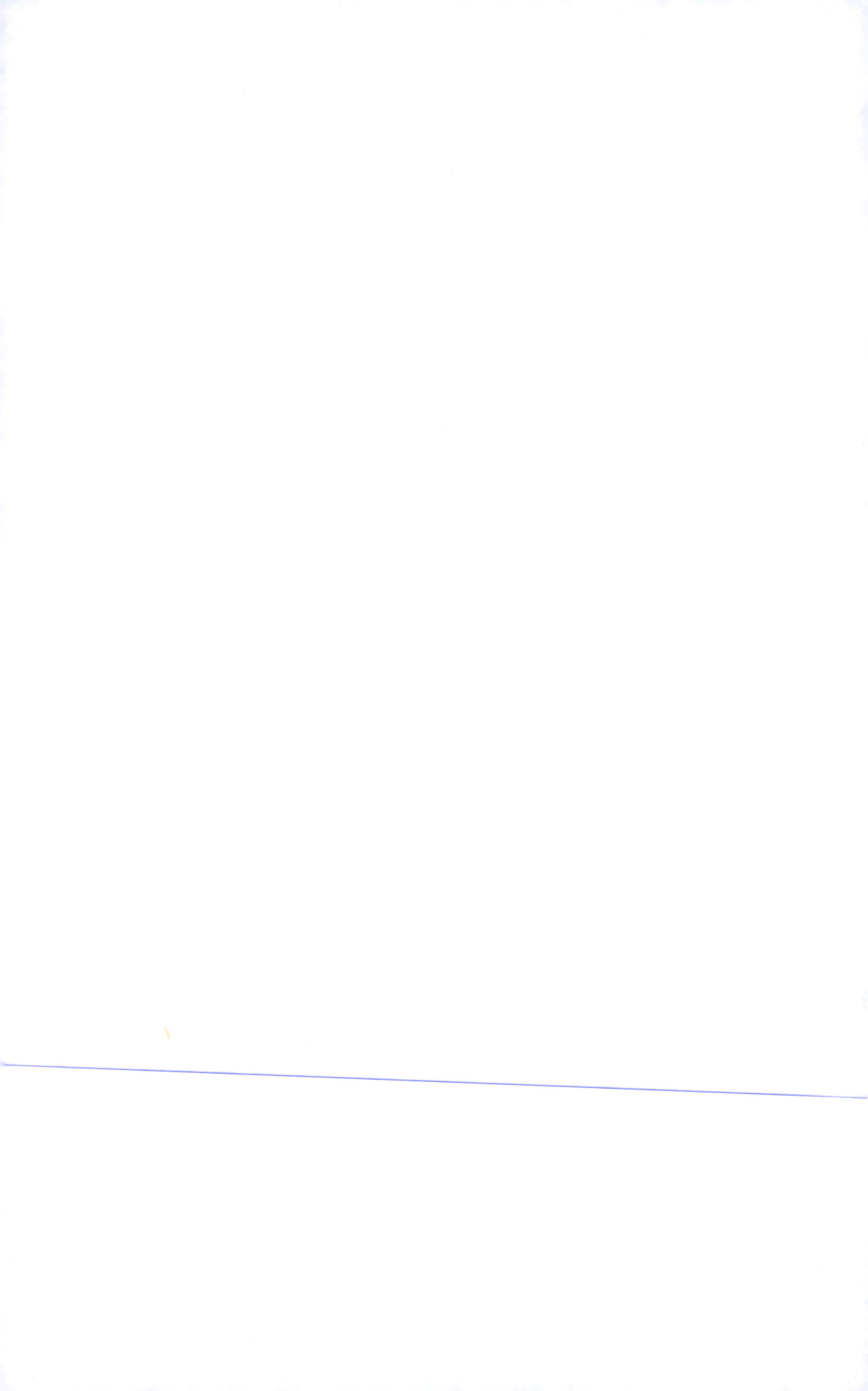

9 7 8 1 5 3 1 6 1 9 3 3 6